Houghton
Mifflin
Harcourt

D1708138

Spelling

Grade 1

ISBN 978-0-544-26778-7

4 5 6 7 8 9 10   0982   22 21 20 19 18 17 16

4500589077   A B C D E F G

Core Skills Spelling

Grade 1

Introduction

Core Skills Spelling is a research-based, systematic spelling program developed to help students master spelling. The program is based on three critical goals for students:

- to learn to spell common spelling patterns and troublesome words
- to learn strategies related to sounds and spelling patterns
- to link spelling and meaning

Each book in the *Core Skills Spelling* program is composed of 30 skill lessons. The majority of skill lessons in this program focus on spellings of vowel sounds. Other skill lessons focus on word structure and content-area words.

Key features of this book include:

- study steps that focus learning,
- lessons that build competency and provide visual reinforcement,
- word study that expands vocabulary and meaning, and
- engaging vocabulary and context activities that encourage students to explore word meanings and use words in meaningful contexts.

Study Steps to Learn a Word

1. **Say** the word. What consonant sounds do you hear? What vowel sounds do you hear? How many syllables do you hear?

2. **Look** at the letters in the word. Think about how each sound is spelled. Find any spelling patterns or parts that you know. Close your eyes. Picture the word in your mind.

3. **Spell** the word aloud.

4. **Write** the word. Say each letter as you write it.

5. **Check** the spelling. If you did not spell the word correctly, use the study steps again.

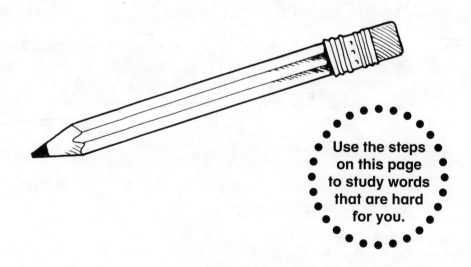

Use the steps on this page to study words that are hard for you.

Spelling Table

Consonants

Sound	Example Words	Spellings
b	big	b
ch	child, catch	ch tch
d	day, add	d dd
f	fast, off	f ff
g	get, egg	g gg
h	hand, who	h wh
j	jog, sponge	j g
k	can, keep, school, sick	c k ch ck
ks	six	x
kw	quit	qu
l	look, all	l ll
m	made, swimming, numb	m mm mb
n	not, running, knock	n nn kn
ng	thank, ring	n ng
p	pet, dropped	p pp
r	run, writer	r wr
s	sat, dress, city	s ss c
sh	she	sh
t	ten, matter	t tt
th	that, thing	th
v	have, of	v f
w	went, whale, one	w wh o
y	you	y
z	zoo, blizzard, says	z zz s

Vowels

Sound	Example Words	Spellings
short a	cat, have	a a_e
long a	baby, take, play, nail, eight, they	a a_e ay ai eigh ey
ah	father, star	a
short e	red, tread, many, said, says	e ea a ai ay
long e	he, eat, tree, people, belief, very	e ea ee eo ie y
short i	is, give	i i_e
long i	find, ride, pie, high, my, eye	i i_e ie igh y eye
short o	on, want	o a
long o	so, nose, road, boulder, snow	o o_e oa ou ow
oi	boy	oy
aw	off, call, haul, saw	o a au aw
o	corn, store, door, four	o o_e oo ou
long oo	zoo, blue, new, do, you	oo ue ew o ou
short oo	good, could, pull	oo ou u
ow	out, owl	ou ow
short u	run, brother	u o

© Houghton Mifflin Harcourt Publishing Company

Commonly Misspelled Words

about	girl	one	too
am	have	or	two
and	her	our	very
are	him	outside	want
because	his	people	was
came	house	play	went
can	in	said	were
color	into	school	when
every	know	some	with
family	like	teacher	would
friend	little	their	your
friends	me	there	
get	my	they	

Lesson 1: m, d, f, g

mop

Mop begins with the **m** sound. Write **m** if the picture name begins with the **m** sound.

1 	2 	3 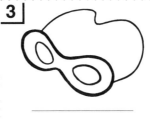	4 
m			

5 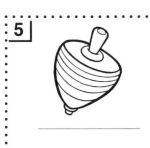	6 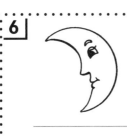	7 	8 

Ham ends with the **m** sound. Write **m** if the picture name ends with the **m** sound.

ham

9 	10 	11 	12 

1

Name _____ Date _____

Dog begins with the **d** sound.
Write **d** if the picture name begins
with the **d** sound.

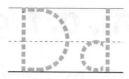

 **d**og

1	2	3	4

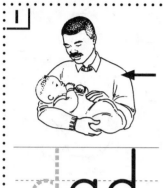 d a d  uck  ig  oll

5	6	7	8

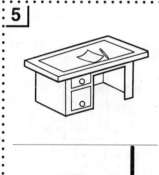 esk 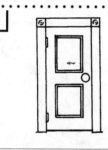 oor  ig  un

---

Bed ends with the **d** sound. Write **d** if the
picture name ends with the **d** sound.

 be**d**

9	10	11	12

 li sa ca   roa

2

Name _____ Date _____

Fan begins with the **f** sound.
Write **f** if the picture name begins
with the **f** sound.

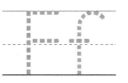

fan

1 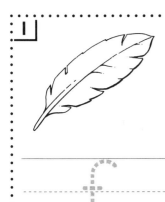	2 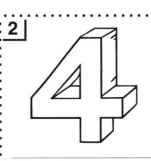	3 	4 
f			

5 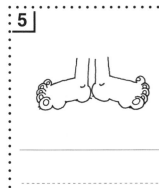	6 	7 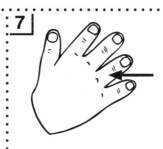	8 

Beef ends with the **f** sound. Write **f** if the
picture name ends with the **f** sound.

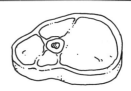
beef

9	10 	11 	12 

3

Gum begins with the **g** sound.
Write **g** if the picture name begins
with the **g** sound.

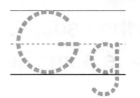
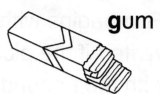

gum

1 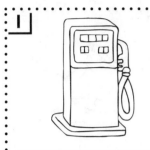	2 	3 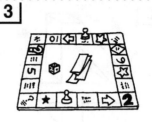	4 
g as	irl	ame	oll

5 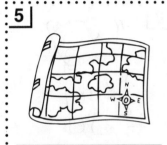	6 	7 	8 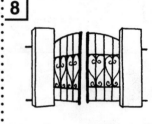
ap	ift	oat	ate

Log ends with the **g** sound. Write **g** if the
picture name ends with the **g** sound.

lo**g**

9 	10 	11 	12 
pi	do	ja	ru

4

Lesson 1
Core Skills Spelling, Grade 1

Name _____ Date _____

Lesson 2: b, t, s, w

Bell begins with the **b** sound.
Write **b** if the picture name begins
with the **b** sound.

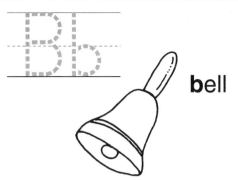

bell

1 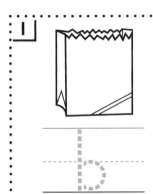 b	2 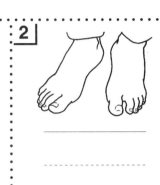	3 	4 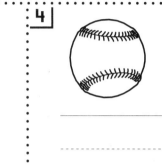
5 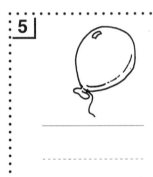	6 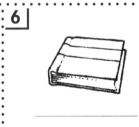	7 	8 

Tub ends with the **b** sound. Write **b** if the
picture name ends with the **b** sound.

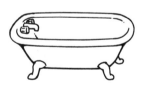

tu**b**

9 	10 	11 	12 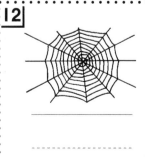

Name _____ Date _____

Ten begins with the **t** sound.
Write **t** if the picture name begins with the **t** sound.

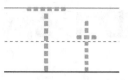

ten

1	2	3	4
		6	7¢
t e n t	u b	i x	a g

5	6	7	8
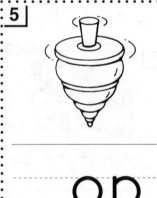	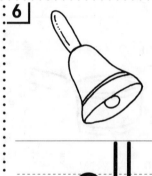		
o p	e l l	o y s	r e e

Net ends with the **t** sound. Write **t** if the picture name ends with the **t** sound.

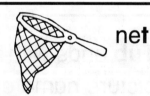

net

9	10	11	12
	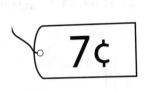	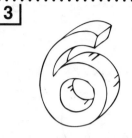	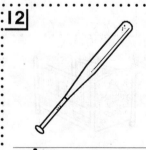
r a	n u	d o	b a

6

Name _____ Date _____

Sun begins with the **s** sound.
Write **s** if the picture name begins
with the **s** sound.

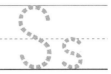 

sun

1 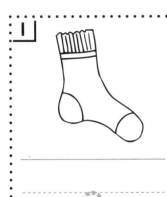	2 	3 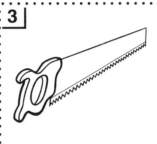	4 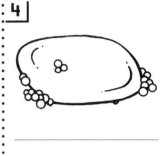
5 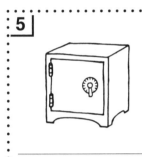	6 	7 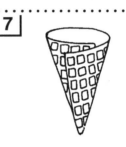	8 

Bus ends with the **s** sound. Write **s** if the
picture name ends with the **s** sound.

 bu**s**

9 	10 	11 	12 

7

Lesson 2
Core Skills Spelling, Grade 1

Name _____ Date _____

Wig begins with the **w** sound.
Write **w** if the picture name
begins with the **w** sound.

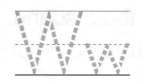
 **w**ig

☐ 1	☐ 2	☐ 3	☐ 4

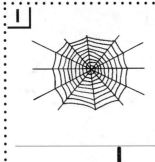

w e b

ox

et

ell

☐ 5	☐ 6	☐ 7	☐ 8

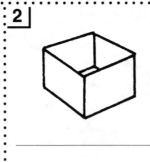

ag

an

ax

ut

☐ 9	☐ 10	☐ 11	☐ 12

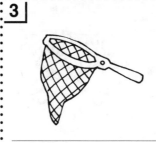

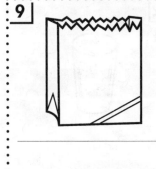

ag

et

in

ask

8

Lesson 2
Core Skills Spelling, Grade 1

Lesson 3: k, j, p, n

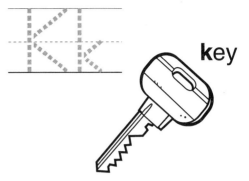
k**ey**

Key begins with the **k** sound.
Write **k** if the picture name begins
with the **k** sound.

1 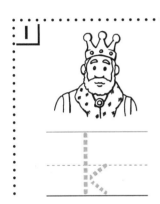	2 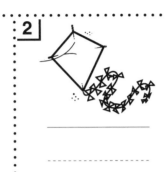	3 	4 
5 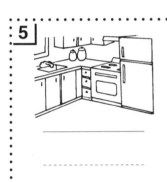	6 	7 	8 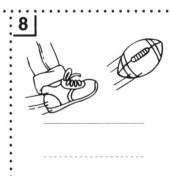

Book ends with the **k** sound. Write **k** if the
picture name ends with the **k** sound.

boo**k**

9	10	11 	12 

Lesson 3
Core Skills Spelling, Grade 1

Name _____ Date _____

Jam begins with the **j** sound.
Write **j** if the picture name begins
with the **j** sound.

 jam

---

| 1 | 2 | 3 | 4 |

 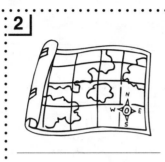  

j ar   ap   j une   ax

| 5 | 6 | 7 | 8 |

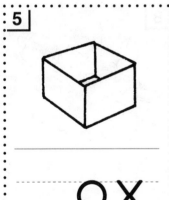   

ox   ug   ip   ump

| 9 | 10 | 11 | 12 |

 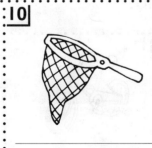 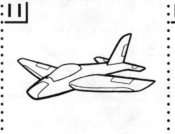 

og   et   et   at

10

Lesson 3
Core Skills Spelling, Grade 1

Name _____ Date _____

Pan begins with the **p** sound.
Write **p** if the picture name begins
with the **p** sound.

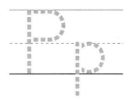  **p**an

1 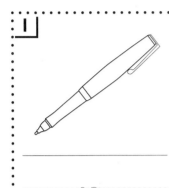	2 	3 	4 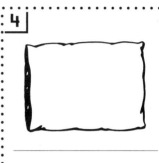

5 	6 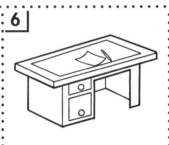	7 	8 

Cup ends with the **p** sound. Write **p** if the
picture name ends with the **p** sound.

 cu**p**

9 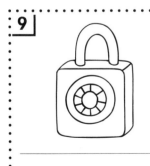	10 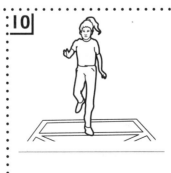	11 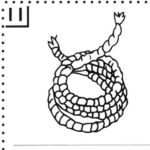	12 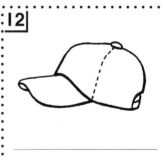

11

Name _____ Date _____

Nut begins with the **n** sound.
Write **n** if the picture name begins
with the **n** sound.

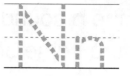

 **n**ut

1 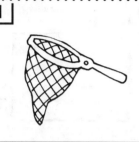	2 	3 	4 
n e t	a p	a i l	u b
5 	6 	7	8
a t	o t e	e s t	o s e

Can ends with the **n** sound. Write **n** if the
picture name ends with the **n** sound.

 can

9 	10 	11 	12 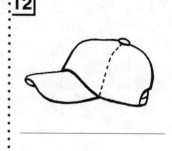
v a	p i	s u	c a

12

Lesson 4: c, h, l, r

cat

Cat begins with the **c** sound.
Write **c** if the picture name begins
with the **c** sound.

1	2	3	4

c			

5	6	7	8

9	10	11	12
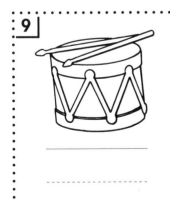			

Name _____ Date _____

Hat begins with the **h** sound.
Write **h** if the picture name begins
with the **h** sound.

  **h**at

1 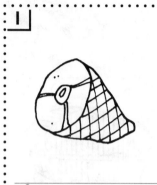	2 	3 	4 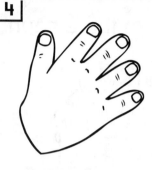
h am	en	ot	and
5 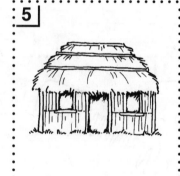	6 	7 	8 
ut	ot	op	ook
9 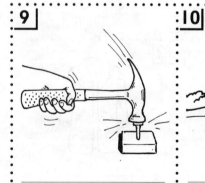	10 	11 	12 
it	ill	orn	at

14

Name _____ Date _____

Lamp begins with the **l** sound.
Write **l** if the picture name begins
with the **l** sound.

 lamp

1 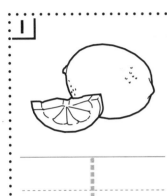	2 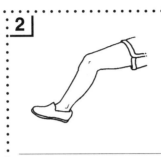	3 	4 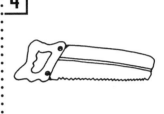
5 	6 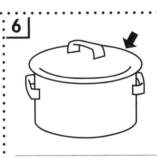	7 	8 

Mail ends with the **l** sound. Write **l** if the
picture name ends with the **l** sound.

 mail

9 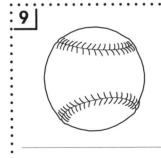	10 	11 	12 

15

Lesson 4
Core Skills Spelling, Grade 1

Name _____   Date _____

Rug begins with the **r** sound.
Write **r** if the picture name
begins with the **r** sound.

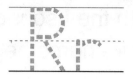  rug

 r un

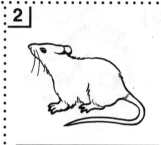 at

| 3 | at |

 ock

 at

 ing

ake

ose

Car ends with the **r** sound. Write **r** if the
picture name ends with the **r** sound.  car

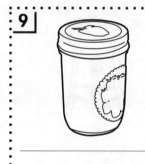 ja

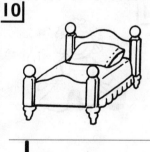 be

 sta

 fou

16

Name _____ Date _____

Lesson 5: v, y, z, qu, x

Vest begins with the **v** sound. Write **v** if the picture name begins with the **v** sound.

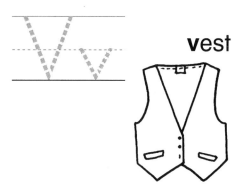 vest

1 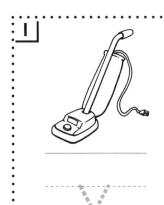	2 	3 	4 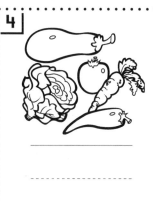
5 	6 	7 	8 
9	10 	11 	12

17

Name _____ Date _____

Yam begins with the **y** sound.
Write **y** if the picture name begins
with the **y** sound.

yam

1	**2**	**3**	**4**

y ell   at   arn   ed

5	**6**	**7**	**8**

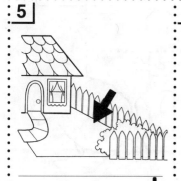 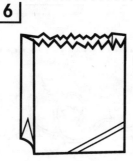  

ard   ag   olk   ig

9	**10**	**11**	**12**

og   awn   in   ak

Lesson 5
Core Skills Spelling, Grade 1

Name _____ Date _____

Zip begins with the **z** sound.
Write **z** if the picture name begins
with the **z** sound.

  zip

1	2	3	4

5	6	7	8
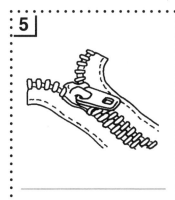			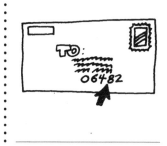

9	10	11	12
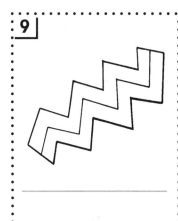	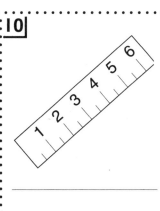		

19

Lesson 5
Core Skills Spelling, Grade 1

Name _____ Date _____

Quilt begins with the **qu** sound. Write **qu** if the picture name begins with the **qu** sound.

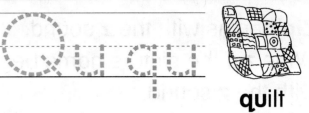

quilt

1	2	3
	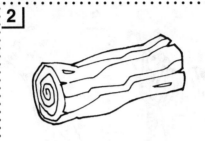	
qu een	__ og	__ art

4	5	6

__ est	__ ack	__ ail

Six ends with the **x** sound. Write **x** if the picture name ends with the **x** sound.

 si**x**

7	8	9	10
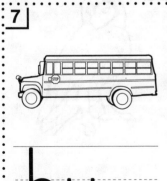	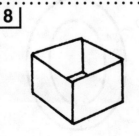		
bu __	bo __	mi __	ya __

Lesson 5
Core Skills Spelling, Grade 1

Name _____   Date _____

Lesson 6: Short a

Cat has the short **a** sound.
Say each picture name.
Write **a** if you hear the short **a** sound.

cat

1 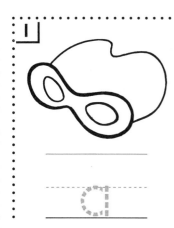 a	**2** 	**3** WELCOME 	**4** 
5 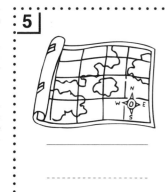	**6** 	**7** 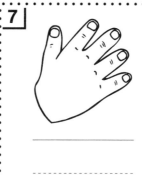	**8** 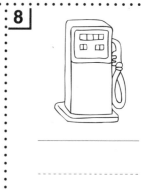
9 	**10** 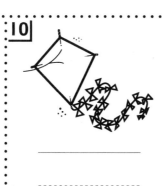	**11** 	**12** 7¢

21

Name _____ Date _____

Say each picture name.
Write **a** if you hear the short **a** sound.
Color each short **a** picture.

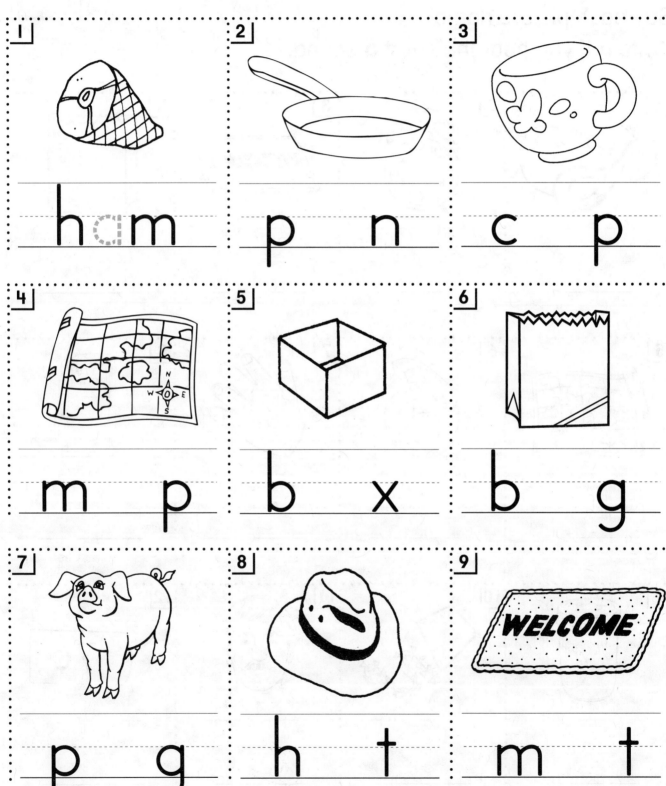

1
h __ m

2
p __ n

3
c __ p

4
m __ p

5
b __ x

6
b __ g

7
p __ g

8
h __ t

9
m __ t

Name _____ Date _____

Say the word that names the first picture.
Circle the pictures whose names rhyme
with the word.

1 pan

2 bag

3 cat

4 cap

5 sad

Lesson 6
Core Skills Spelling, Grade 1

Name _____ Date _____

Say each picture name. Trace the first letter.
Then write **an** to make the word.

1 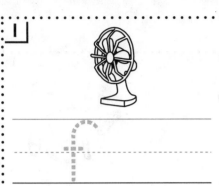	2 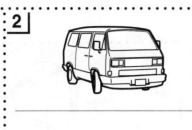	3 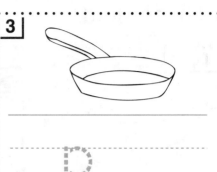
_____	_____	_____
f	v	p

4 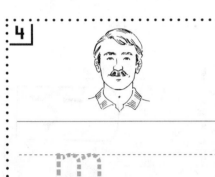	5 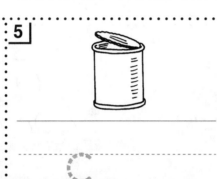	6 
_____	_____	_____
m	c	r

Say each picture name. Trace the first letter.
Then write **at** to make the word.

7 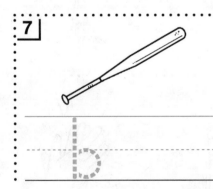	8 	9 
_____	_____	_____
b	c	h

10 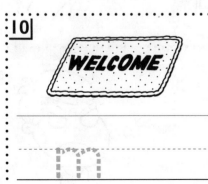	11 	12 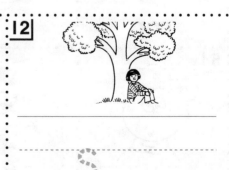
WELCOME		
_____	_____	_____
m	r	s

24

Lesson 7: Short e

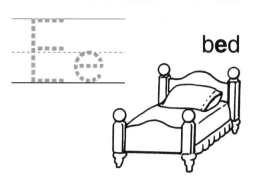

bed

Bed has the short **e** sound.

Say each picture name.

Write **e** if you hear the short **e** sound.

1	2	3	4
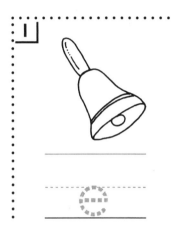		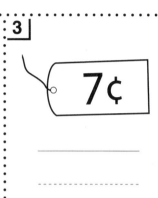	

5	6	7	8

9	10	11	12
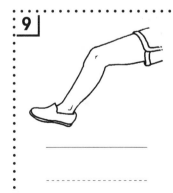	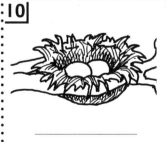		

25

Name _____ Date _____

Say each picture name.

Write **e** if you hear the short **e** sound.

Color each short **e** picture.

1  v __ t	2 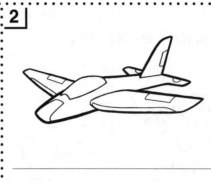 j __ t	3 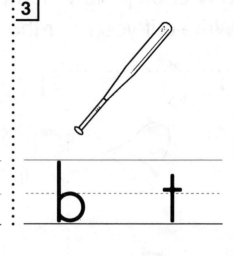 b __ t
4 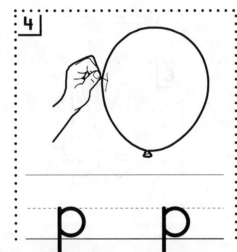 p __ p	5 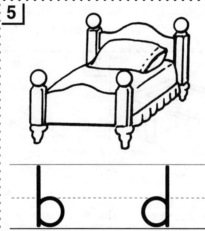 b __ d	6 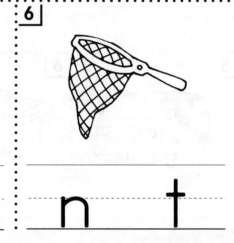 n __ t
7  m __ n	8  h __ p	9 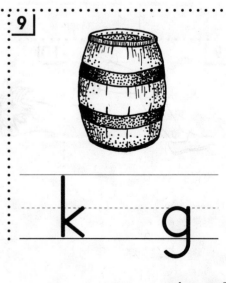 k __ g

26

Name _____ Date _____

Say the word that names the first picture.
Circle the pictures whose names rhyme
with the word.

1			
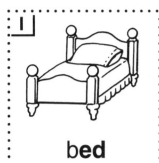 **b**ed			

2			
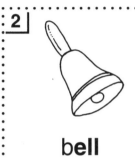 **b**ell			

3			
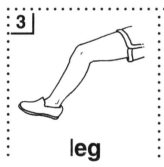 **l**eg			

4			
 **v**et			

5			
 **h**en			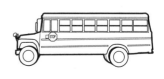

27

Name _____ Date _____

Say each picture name. Trace the first letter.
Then write **ell** to make the word.

1	2	3
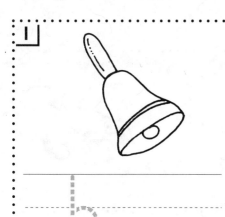	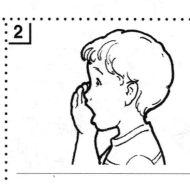	
b___	y___	t___

4	5
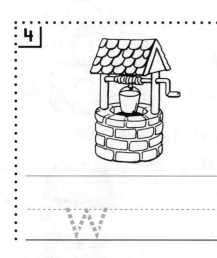	
w___	f___

Say each picture name. Trace the first letter.
Then write **en** to make the word.

6	7	8

h___	m___	t___

Name _____ Date _____

Lesson 8: Short i

Pig has the short **i** sound.

Say each picture name.

Write **i** if you hear the short **i** sound.

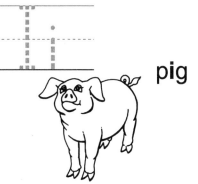

pig

1 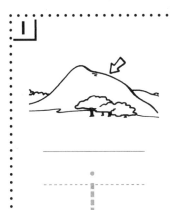	2 	3 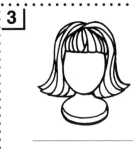	4 
5 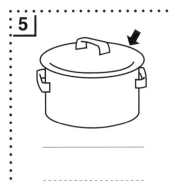	6 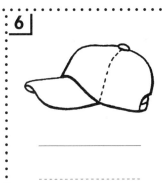	7 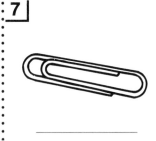	8 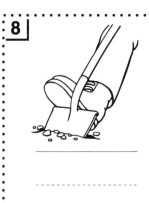
9 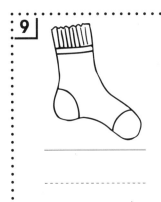	10 	11 	12 

29

Name _____ Date _____

Say each picture name.

Write **i** if you hear the short **i** sound.

Color each short **i** picture.

1	2	3
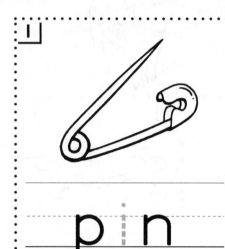		
p i n	f x	p g

4	5	6
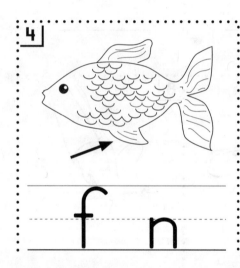		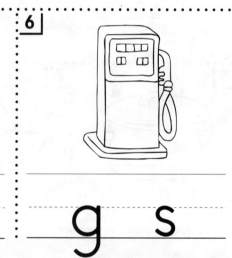
f n	d g	g s

7	8	9
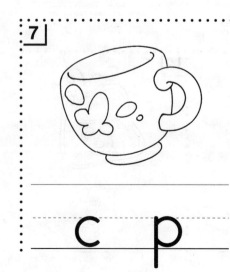		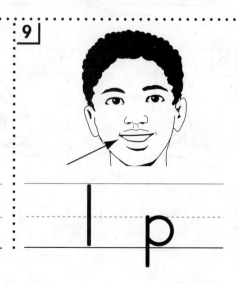
c p	k t	l p

Lesson 8
Core Skills Spelling, Grade 1

Name _____ Date _____

Say the word that names the first picture.
Circle the pictures whose names rhyme
with the word.

1. pin

2. kit

3. lip

4. pig

5. fix

31

Say each picture name. Trace the first letter.
Then write **it** to make the word.

1	2	3
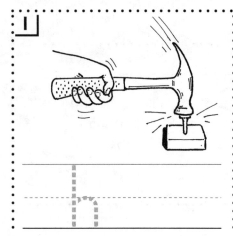	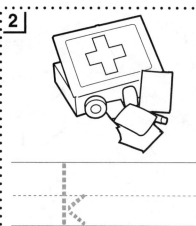	
h	k	s

Say each picture name. Trace the first letter.
Then write **ig** to make the word.

4	5	6
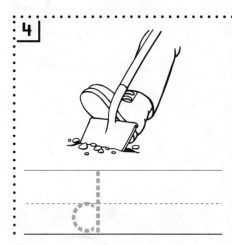		
d	p	w

7		
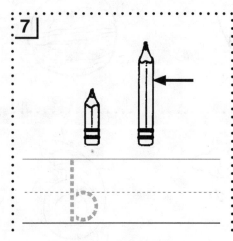		
b		

Name _____ Date _____

Lesson 9: Short o

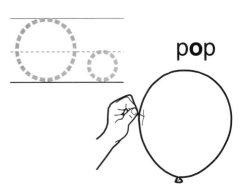

p**o**p

Pop has the short **o** sound.
Say each picture name.
Write **o** if you hear the short **o** sound.

1	2	3	4

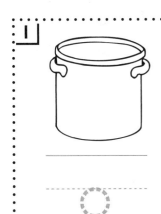 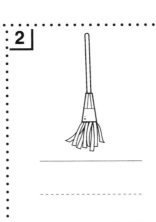  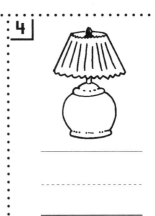

5	6	7	8

 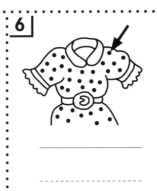 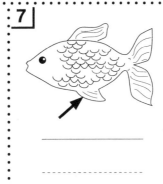 

9	10	11	12

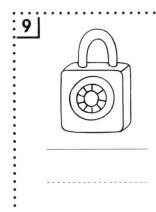  

33

Name _____ Date _____

Say each picture name.

Write **o** if you hear the short **o** sound.

Color each short **o** picture.

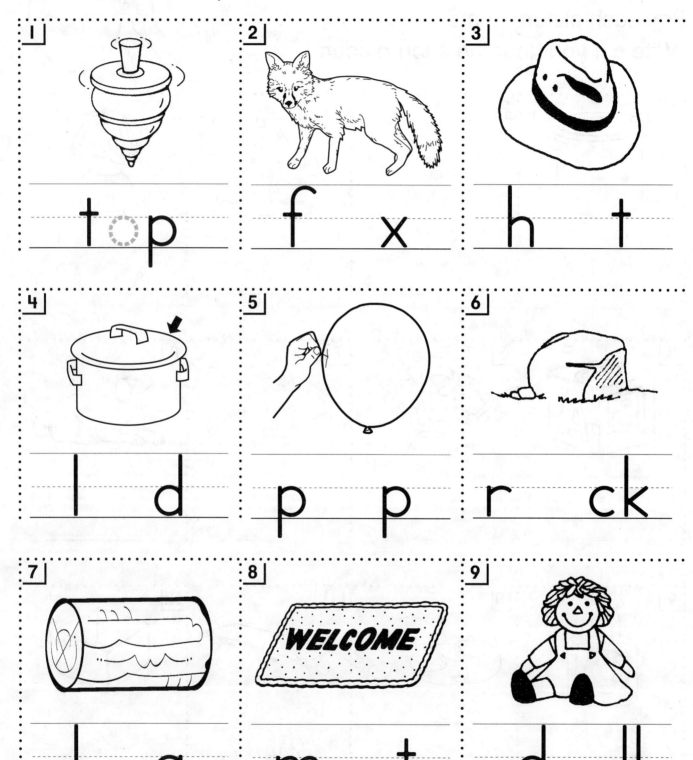

1   t o p

2   f   x

3   h   t

4   l   d

5   p   p

6   r   ck

7   l   g

8   m   t

9   d   ll

34

Name _____ Date _____

Say the word that names the first picture.
Circle the pictures whose names rhyme
with the word.

1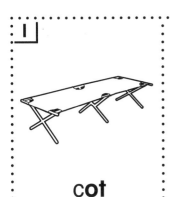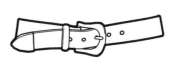

cot

2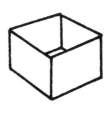

fox

3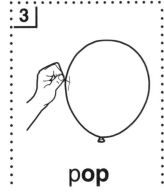

pop

4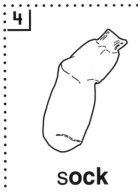

sock

35

Name _____ Date _____

Say each picture name. Trace the first letter.
Then write **op** to make the word.

1 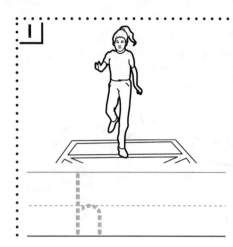	2 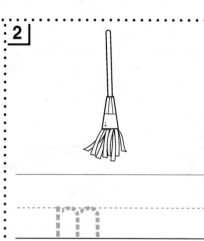	3 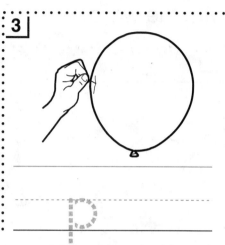
h	m	p

Say each picture name. Trace the first letter.
Then write **ot** to make the word.

4 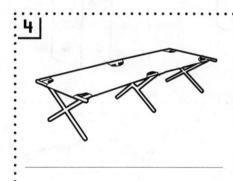	5 	6 
c	d	h

7 
p

36

Name _____ Date _____

Lesson 10: Short u

Cup has the short **u** sound.
Say each picture name.
Write **u** if you hear the short **u** sound.

 c**u**p

| 1 | 2 | 3 | 4 |

_____ _____ _____ _____

u

| 5 | 6 | 7 | 8 |

      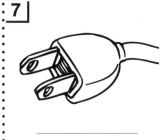   

_____ _____ _____ _____

| 9 | 10 | 11 | 12 |

_____ _____ _____ _____

37

Name _____   Date _____

Say each picture name.

Write **u** if you hear the short **u** sound.

Color each short **u** picture.

1	2	3

c u p	p _ p	h _ n

4	5	6

s _ n	b _ b	c _ b

7	8	9

r _ g	j _ m	n _ t

38

Lesson 10
Core Skills Spelling, Grade 1

Name _____ Date _____

Say the word that names the first picture.
Circle the pictures whose names rhyme
with the word.

1  **hut**			
2  **sun**		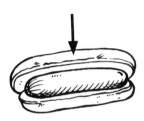	
3  **tub**			
4  **gum**			
5  **rug**			

39

Name _____ Date _____

Say each picture name. Trace the first letter.
Then write **ug** to make the word.

1	2	3

m	h	j

4	5	6
		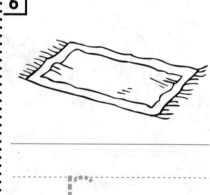
b	t	r

Say each picture name. Trace the first letter.
Then write **ut** to make the word.

7	8	9
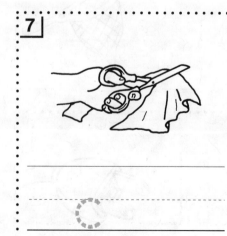	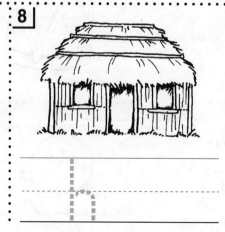	
c	h	n

40

Name _____ Date _____

Lesson 11: Words with Short a

Say and Write

1. am

2. at

3. can

4. ran

5. fast

6. last

The short **a** sound can be spelled **a**.

ran

fast

Lesson 11
Core Skills Spelling, Grade 1

Spell and Write

Write the spelling word that completes each sentence.

am	ran
at	fast
can	last

1. I _____ Sam.

2. A duck _____ swim.

3. The dog is _____ the farm.

4. The pig _____ with her.

5. My dog can run _____.

6. The cat is _____.

Name _____ Date _____

Read and Write

Write the spelling words to complete
the story.

am   ran
at   fast
can   last

_____

Randy Rabbit _____ on a path. The path

was _____ the park. Randy ran well. He ran

_____. That was _____ week.

Now he will run again. "I _____ ready," Randy

says. "I _____ do it!"

43

Name _____ Date _____

Practice
Write the letter that completes each
spelling word.

1. r ___ n

2. l ___ st

3. ___ m

4. ___ t

5. c ___ n

6. f ___ st

Write the words you made.

1. _____

2. _____

3. _____

4. _____

5. _____

6. _____

Name _____ Date _____

Lesson 12: More Words with Short a

Study Steps
1. Say
2. Look
3. Spell
4. Write
5. Check

Say and Write

1.  sat _____

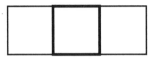

2.  van _____

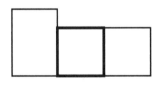

3.  has _____

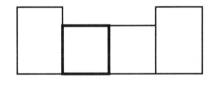

4.  hand _____

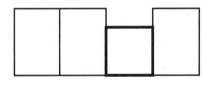

5.  that _____

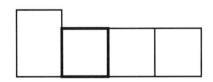

6. have _____

The short **a** sound can be spelled **a**.

van   hand

Lesson 12
Core Skills Spelling, Grade 1

Name _____ Date _____

Spell and Write

Write the spelling word that completes
each sentence.

sat	hand
van	that
has	have

1. Pam has a _____ .

2. Will you get _____ for me?

3. Jan can draw her _____ .

4. Dan _____ by his pal.

5. Hal and Jack _____ caps.

6. My cat _____ a ball.

46

Lesson 12
Core Skills Spelling, Grade 1

Name _____   Date _____

Read and Write

Write the spelling words to complete
the story.

sat   hand
van   that
has   have

Nan _____ with her dad. Nan

had a book in her _____. She got it

from Books on Wheels. Books on Wheels is

a _____. It _____ many good

books in it. Nan likes _____ van. Do you

_____ Books on Wheels where you live?

47

© Houghton Mifflin Harcourt Publishing Company

Lesson 12
Core Skills Spelling, Grade 1

Name _____ Date _____

Practice

Change each letter in dark type to make a spelling word.

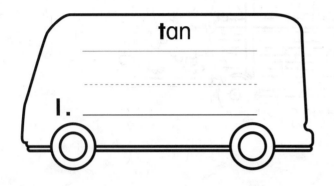

tan

1. _____

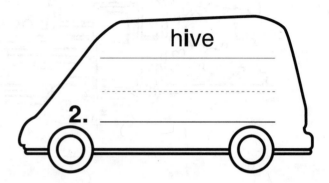

hive

2. _____

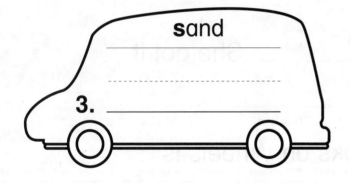

sand

3. _____

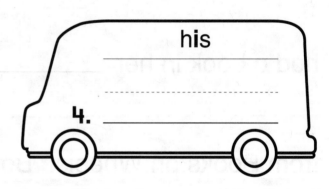

his

4. _____

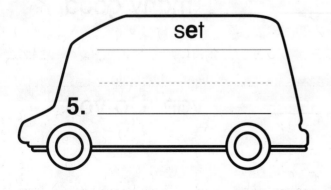

s**e**t

5. _____

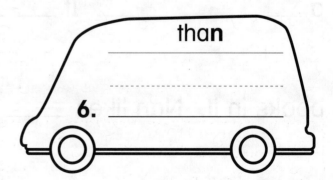

tha**n**

6. _____

Name _____ Date _____

Lesson 13: Words with Short e

Study Steps
1. Say
2. Look
3. Spell
4. Write
5. Check

Say and Write

1.  end

2.  ten

3.  red

4.  wet

5.  tell

6.  seven

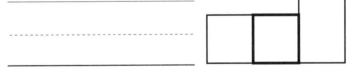

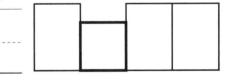

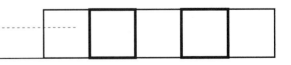

The short **e** sound can be spelled **e**.

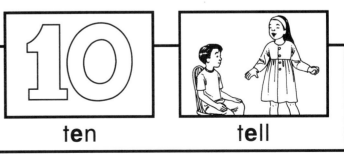

ten   tell

Lesson 13
Core Skills Spelling, Grade 1

Name _____ Date _____

Spell and Write

Write the spelling word that completes
each sentence.

1.   The dog is _____ .

2.   A rose is the color _____ .

3.   Five plus five is _____ .

4.   I am at the _____ of the line.

5.   There are _____ bees.

6.   Mr. Silva will _____ a story.

Read and Write
Write the spelling
words to complete
the story.

Rex washes his socks. Some are _____.

Some are white. The socks are dripping

_____

_____. Rex puts them on the line.

He has five pairs. There are _____ socks

on the line. Three socks on the _____ fall.

Now only _____ socks are on the line.

Who will _____ Rex?

Name _____ Date _____

Practice

Write the spelling word for each clue.
Use the letters in the boxes to solve
the riddle.

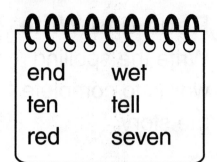

end   wet
ten   tell
red   seven

1. say = ___ ___ □ ___

2. 1 + 6 = ___ □ ___ ___ ___

3. 5 + 5 = □ ___ ___

4. not dry = ___ ___ □

5. the last part = □ ___ ___

6. a color = □ ___ ___

You can find me in the <u>ABC</u>s. What am I?

a _____

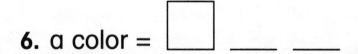

Lesson 13
Core Skills Spelling, Grade 1

Name _____ Date _____

Lesson 14: More Words with Short e

Study Steps
1. Say
2. Look
3. Spell
4. Write
5. Check

Say and Write

1.  _____

2.  _____

3.  _____

4.  _____

5.  _____

6.  _____

The short **e** sound can be spelled **e**.

p**e**t

h**e**lp

Lesson 14
Core Skills Spelling, Grade 1

Spell and Write

Write the spelling word that completes
each sentence.

get	went
pet	best
help	when

1. Brett's _____ is a dog.

2. My cat naps _____ it is hot.

3. This dog is the _____!

4. Mom _____ to the store.

5. Ted and Jen _____ the balls.

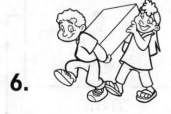

6. Ken can _____ Beth.

Name _____ Date _____

Read and Write
Write the spelling words
to complete the story.

_____

A puppy is a good _____. Would

_____

you like to _____ a puppy? You can

_____

_____ take care of it. You can feed your

_____

puppy _____ it is hungry. You can play with

_____

it. You will wonder where the time _____.

_____

Do you think a puppy is the _____ pet?

55

Practice

Change each letter in dark type to
make a spelling word.

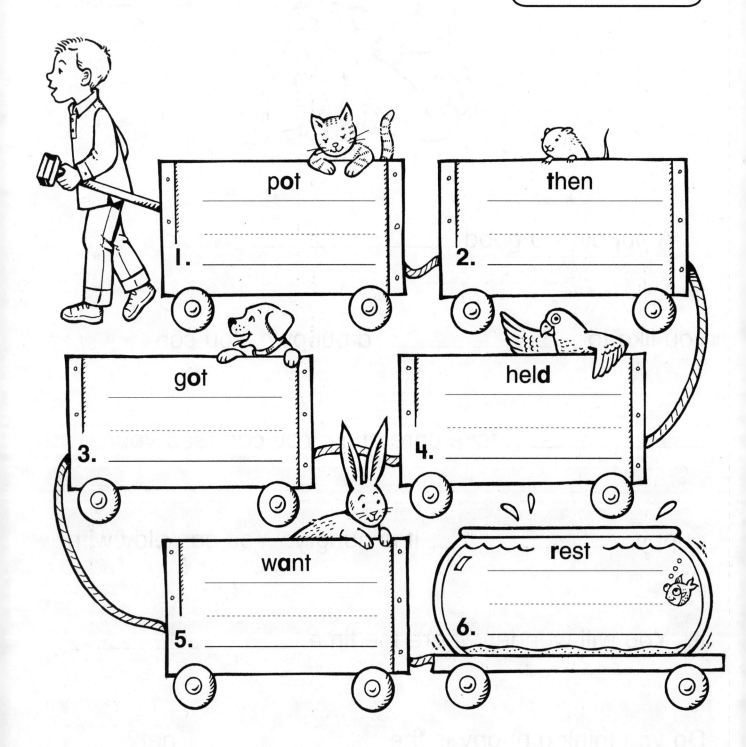

pot

1. _____

then

2. _____

g**o**t

3. _____

hel**d**

4. _____

w**a**nt

5. _____

rest

6. _____

Lesson 14
Core Skills Spelling, Grade 1

Name _____   Date _____

Lesson 15: Words with Short i

Study Steps
1. Say
2. Look
3. Spell
4. Write
5. Check

Say and Write

1. in _____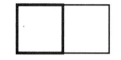

2. is _____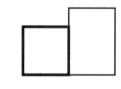

3. it _____

4. with _____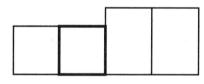

5. sick _____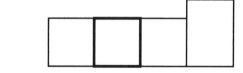

6. quit _____

The short **i** sound can be spelled **i**.

in   sick

Name _____ Date _____

Spell and Write

Write the spelling word that completes
each sentence.

1. Nick feels _____.

2. I have milk _____ my food.

3. He _____ happy.

4. Lee plays _____ the sand.

5. Jenny wants the rain to _____.

6. The flower has a bee on _____.

© Houghton Mifflin Harcourt Publishing Company

Lesson 15
Core Skills Spelling, Grade 1

Read and Write

Write the spelling words to complete
the selection.

in	with
is	sick
it	quit

Sometimes people get _____. Then they must

stay _____ bed. It _____ not much fun.

You can make a picture for a sick friend. Get some paper.

Draw on _____. Paint on it _____ bright

colors. Don't _____ until it looks great. Give it to

your friend. Say, "Get well quick!"

Name _____   Date _____

Practice

Write the missing spelling words.

in	with
is	sick
it	quit

Don't be _____.
Get well quick!

1. _____

We will go _____.

2. _____

Jim,
Will you play
with me when
school _____
out?

3. _____

Don't
_____ now!

4. _____

Drink milk
_____ lunch.

5. _____

Put _____ in
the can!

6. _____

60

Name _____ Date _____

Lesson 16: More Words with Short i

Study Steps
1. Say
2. Look
3. Spell
4. Write
5. Check

Say and Write

1. if _____

2. six _____

3. sit _____

4. big _____

5. did _____

6. this _____

The short **i** sound can be spelled **i**.

six   big

Lesson 16
Core Skills Spelling, Grade 1

Name _____ Date _____

Spell and Write

Write the spelling word that completes
each sentence.

1. Milly has _____ puppies.

2. We will get wet _____ it rains.

3. We _____ together.

4. The _____ box has many toys.

5. Dad and I _____ the shopping.

6. I drew all of _____.

Name _____ Date _____

Read and Write

Write the spelling words to complete the story.

if	big
six	did
sit	this

_____

I have _____ little kittens. My kittens will not

_____

always be little. Soon they will be _____. The

_____

kittens _____ on me. They go to sleep

_____

in my lap. They wake up _____ I move.

_____

Then _____ is what they do. They cry,

_____

"Mew! Mew!" They _____ it just now!

Name _____ Date _____

Practice

Write the letter or letters that complete each spelling word.

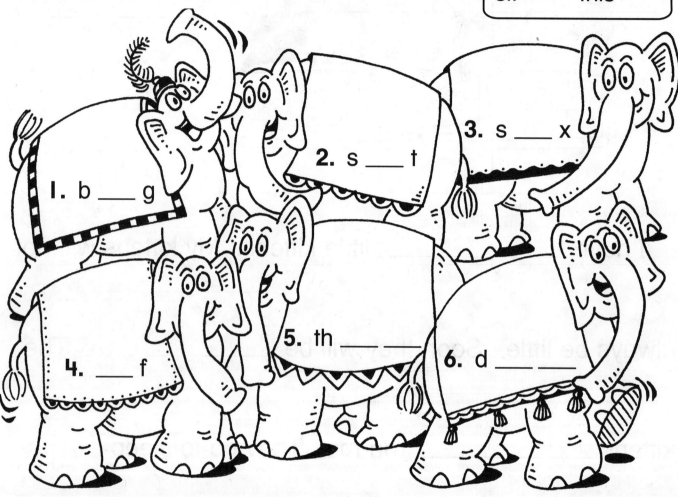

1. b ___ g

2. s ___ t

3. s ___ x

4. ___ f

5. th ___

6. d ___

Write the words you made.

1. _____   2. _____   3. _____

4. _____   5. _____   6. _____

64

Name _____ Date _____

Lesson 17: Words with Short o

Say and Write

1. on

2. top

3. not

4. hop

5. hot

6. stop

The short **o** sound can be spelled **o**.

 hop

STOP

stop

Lesson 17
Core Skills Spelling, Grade 1

Spell and Write

Write the spelling word that completes each sentence.

on	hop
top	hot
not	stop

1. _____

   _____

   A frog can _____.

2. _____

   _____

   We must _____ and wait.

3. _____

   _____

   The lamp is _____ the table.

4. _____

   _____

   Don is _____.

5. _____

   _____

   My dog will _____ stop.

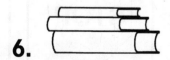

6. _____

   _____

   The little book is on _____.

Read and Write

Write the spelling words to complete
the story.

on	hop
top	hot
not	stop

_____

Bonnie likes to _____. She hops and hops.

_____

Bonnie hops _____ the path. She hops on

_____

the grass. She does _____ fall. Then she

_____

hops to the _____ of the hill. When will Bonnie

_____

_____? She will have to stop when she gets

_____

too _____!

67

Name _____ Date _____

Practice

Change each letter in dark type to make a spelling word.

on	hop
top	hot
not	stop

hat

1. _____

in

2. _____

tap

3. _____

net

4. _____

st**e**p

5. _____

hip

6. _____

68

© Houghton Mifflin Harcourt Publishing Company

Lesson 17
Core Skills Spelling, Grade 1

Name _____ Date _____

Lesson 18: More Words with Short o

Say and Write

1. fox _____

2. mop _____

3. job _____

4. box _____

5. lock _____

6. sock _____

The short **o** sound can be spelled **o**.

fox

sock

69

Lesson 18
Core Skills Spelling, Grade 1

Name _____ Date _____

Spell and Write

Write the spelling word that completes
each sentence.

1. Ron lost a _____ .

2. Bob can _____ up the mess.

3. Mom has a _____ at school.

4. A _____ lives in the woods.

5. He put a key in the _____ .

6. The toys go in a _____ .

Name _____ Date _____

Read and Write

Write the spelling words
to complete the story.

_____

Bob the Ox had a _____ to do. He had to

_____   _____

_____. A _____ came in. He had a

_____

_____. The fox took out a brush. "Put this on

_____

your _____," he said.

Bob did it. Then he put a brush on his other sock.

He started to mop. "This is fast!" Bob said. "Soon I can

_____

_____ up and go have fun!"

71

Practice

Help each fox find its home. Draw lines from the foxes to the dens to make the spelling words.

fox	box
mop	lock
job	sock

Write the words you made.

1. _____

2. _____

3. _____

4. _____

5. _____

6. _____

Name _____ Date _____

Lesson 19: Words with Short u

Study Steps
1. Say
2. Look
3. Spell
4. Write
5. Check

Say and Write

1. us _____

2. run _____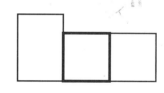

3. fun _____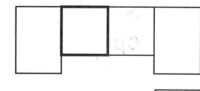

4. jump _____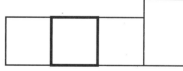

5. much _____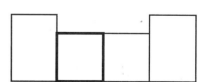

6. duck _____

The short **u** sound can be spelled **u**.

r**u**n   d**u**ck

73

Spell and Write

Write the spelling word that completes
each sentence.

us	jump
run	much
fun	duck

1.   Bud walks with _____.

2.   He can _____ fast.

3.   Meg and Sally _____ rope.

4.   He feeds the _____.

5.   Josh and Jill had _____.

6.   How _____ will Mom read?

Name _____ Date _____

Read and Write

Write the spelling words to complete
the story.

us	jump
run	much
fun	duck

A baby _____ is called a duckling. A

duckling cannot _____ fast. But it can have

_____

_____. It can _____ into the water.

It can swim, too. The mother duck quacks if a duckling

swims too far away. She is saying, "You have gone

_____   _____

_____ too far. Come back to _____!"

75

Name _____ Date _____

Practice

Write the letter or letters that
complete each spelling word.

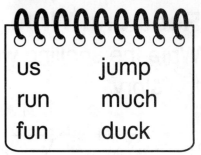

us   jump

run   much

fun   duck

1.  j ___ ___ p

2. 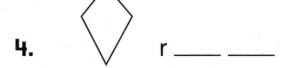 ___ ___ ch

3.  f ___ n

4. ◇ r ___ ___

5. ☐ d ___ ck

6. ⬭ ___ s

___

Match each object with a shape above. Write
the word you made that is next to the shape.

7. 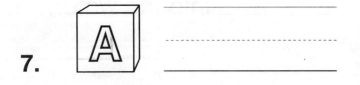 _____

8.  _____

9. 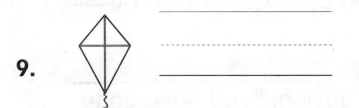 _____

10. 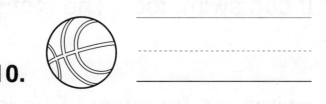 _____

11. 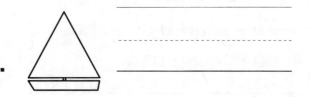 _____

12. 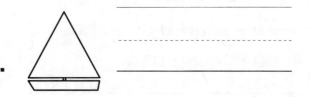 _____

76

Name _____ Date _____

Lesson 20: More Words with Short u

Study Steps
1. Say
2. Look
3. Spell
4. Write
5. Check

Say and Write

1. up

2. cut

3. bus

4. but

5. must

6. just

The short **u** sound can be spelled **u**.

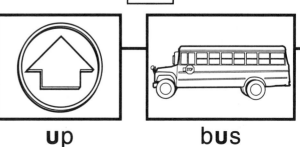

up   b**u**s

Name _____ Date _____

Spell and Write

Write the spelling word that completes
each sentence.

1. _____

    She will ride the _____.

2. _____

    Cindy _____ pick up the toys.

3. _____

    Sunny will _____ the rope.

4. _____

    The girls look _____ alike.

5. _____

    It is cold, _____ there is no snow.

6. _____

    The ball goes _____ and down.

Name _____   Date _____

Read and Write

Write the spelling words to complete
the selection.

SCHOOL BUS

up	but
cut	must
bus	just

Do you know what to do on a _____? You

_____ sit down when the bus is moving. You

cannot stand _____. You can play a game.

You can sing a song, too. You can draw, _____

do not use scissors. You might _____ yourself.

You can read, or you can _____ sit and rest.

79

Name _____   Date _____

Practice

Write the letter that completes each spelling word.

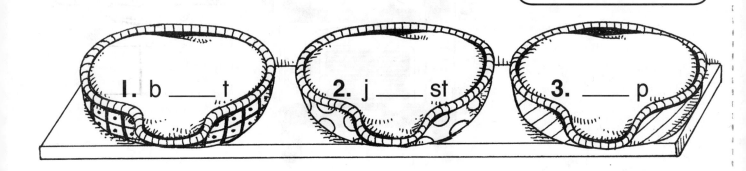

1. b ___ t   2. j ___ st   3. ___ p

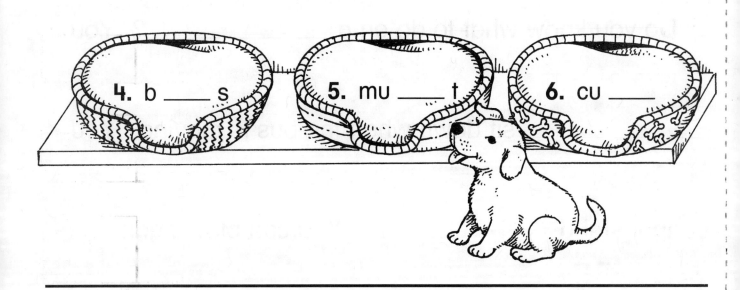

4. b ___ s   5. mu ___ t   6. cu ___

Write the words you made.

1. _____   2. _____   3. _____

4. _____   5. _____   6. _____

80

Name _____ Date _____

Lesson 21: Words with Long a

Study Steps
1. Say
2. Look
3. Spell
4. Write
5. Check

Say and Write

1. name _____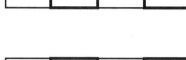

2. game _____

3. same _____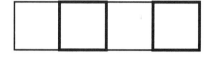

4. made _____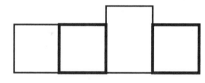

5. make _____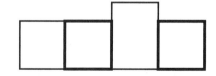

6. take _____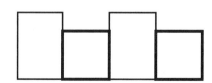

The long **a** sound can be spelled **a__e**.

g**a**m**e**

t**a**k**e**

Lesson 21
Core Skills Spelling, Grade 1

Name _____   Date _____

Spell and Write

Write the spelling word that completes
each sentence.

1. John will _____ a snack.

2. Jake and Kate play a _____.

3. The cat's _____ is Gabe.

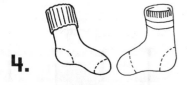

4. Are the socks the _____?

5. Jade will _____ her lunch.

6. Tate _____ a plane.

Lesson 21
Core Skills Spelling, Grade 1

Name _____ Date _____

Read and Write

Write the spelling words
to complete the selection.

name	made
game	make
same	take

Sal sails on the sea some Saturdays.

What is your _____? Play a _____

with your name. To begin _____ the first letter

of your name, such as **S**. Think of words that begin

with the _____ letter. Next _____ a

sentence with the words. Then add more words to the

sentence you _____.

Name _____ Date _____

Practice

Draw lines from the cakes to the
plates to make the spelling words.

name	made
game	make
same	take

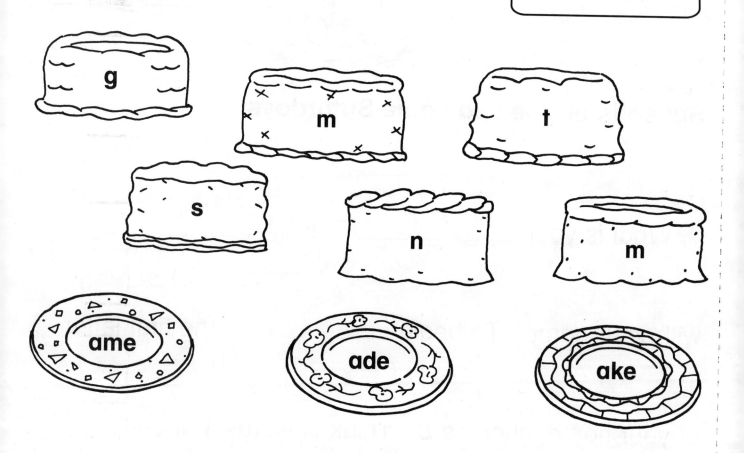

g

m

t

s

n

m

ame

ade

ake

Write the words you made.

1. _____

2. _____

3. _____

4. _____

5. _____

6. _____

84

© Houghton Mifflin Harcourt Publishing Company

Lesson 21
Core Skills Spelling, Grade 1

Name _____ Date _____

Lesson 22: More Words with Long a

Study Steps
1. Say
2. Look
3. Spell
4. Write
5. Check

Say and Write

1.  day _____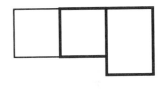

2.  may _____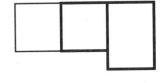

3. say _____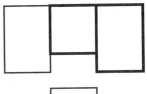

4.  pay _____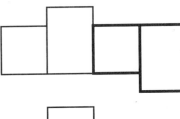

5.  stay _____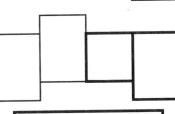

6. play _____

The long **a** sound can be spelled **ay**.

p**ay**   pl**ay**

Name _____ Date _____

Spell and Write

Write the spelling word that completes
each sentence.

day   pay
may   stay
say   play

1. Mom will _____ for the shoes.

2. It is a nice _____.

3. Fay must _____ in bed.

4. He _____ get wet today.

5. The kitten likes to _____.

6. What will Mom _____?

86

Read and Write

Write the spelling words to complete
the selection.

day	pay
may	stay
say	play

Some work places have a special _____.

Children _____ go to work with an adult. They

can _____ all day. They learn about jobs.

They have fun, but it is not a time to _____.

The children _____ they learn a lot. They see

how adults work for their _____.

Name _____ Date _____

Practice

Write the spelling words to answer
the questions.

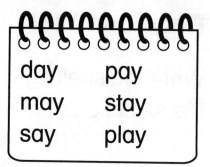
1. What can you
do with a ball?

2. When are you
awake?

3. Which word
means **don't
go**?

4. What must you
do when you
buy?

5. What do you do
when you talk?

6. Which word
means **might**?

 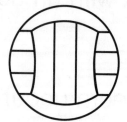  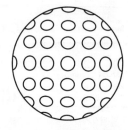 

1. _____

2. _____

3. _____

4. _____

5. _____

6. _____

Name _____ Date _____

Lesson 23: Words with Long e

Study Steps
1. Say
2. Look
3. Spell
4. Write
5. Check

Say and Write

1.  _____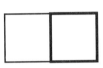

2.  _____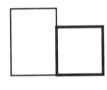

3.  _____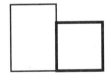

4.  _____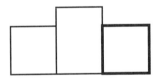

5.  _____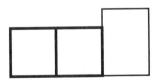

6.  _____

The long **e** sound can be spelled **e** or **ea**.

we

eat

Lesson 23
Core Skills Spelling, Grade 1

Name _____ Date _____

Spell and Write

Write the spelling word that completes
each sentence.

1. "Are _____ late?" Lee asked.

2. It is time to _____.

3. Is _____ calling Mom?

4. "Will you help _____?" he asked.

5. She will _____ awake soon.

6. Will _____ wake up and play?

Lesson 23
Core Skills Spelling, Grade 1

Name _____ Date _____

Read and Write

Write the spelling words to complete
the story.

me   she
we   eat
he
be

My family sleeps a lot in winter. We need food

_____   _____

before _____ sleep. We _____ a

_____

lot! Today Mom showed _____ how to catch

_____

fish. Then _____ showed my brother. I know

_____

_____ likes fish. Soon we will find a cave.

_____

A cave is a good place to _____ in winter.

91

Lesson 23
Core Skills Spelling, Grade 1

Name _____ Date _____

Practice

Write the letter or letters that
complete each spelling word.

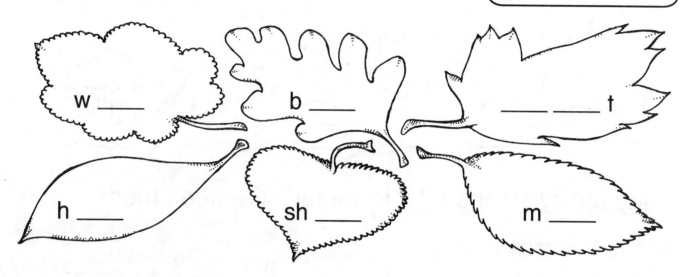

w ____   b ____   ___ ___ t

h ____   sh ____   m ____

Find the matching leaf above. Write the word from that leaf.

1. _____

2. _____

3.

4.

5.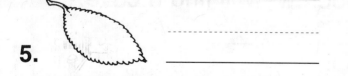

6. _____

92

© Houghton Mifflin Harcourt Publishing Company

Lesson 24: More Words with Long e

Study Steps
1. Say
2. Look
3. Spell
4. Write
5. Check

Say and Write

1. see _____

2. feet _____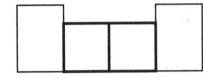

3. keep _____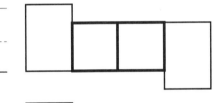

4. tree _____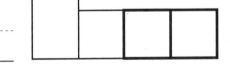

5. street _____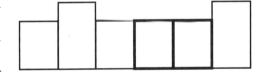

6. three _____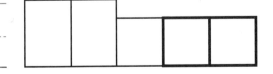

The long **e** sound can be spelled **ee**.

tree

street

Spell and Write

Write the spelling word that completes each sentence.

see   tree
feet   street
keep   three

1. Leaves fell from the _____.

2. They walk across the _____.

3. This thing has many _____.

4. What does she _____?

5. Pete can _____ the gift.

6. The _____ kittens play all day.

Name _____ Date _____

Read and Write

Write the spelling words to
complete the story.

Dee's dad took her on a hike with _____

_____

of her friends. They all live on the same _____.

"Please _____ walking on the trail," Dad said.

Something went splash! "What is on the other side of that

_____?" Dad asked.

"I _____ a creek!" Lee said. "Some kids are

in the water. May we get our _____ wet, too?"

95

Name _____   Date _____

Practice

Write the letters that complete each spelling word.

1. str ___ ___ ___

2. tr ___ ___ ___

3. thr ___ ___

4. s ___ ___

5. Please
   k ___ ___ ___
   off the grass!

6. f ___ ___ ___

Write the words you made.

1. _____

2. _____

3. _____

4. _____

5. _____

6. _____

96

Name _____ Date _____

Lesson 25: Words with Long i

Say and Write

Study Steps
1. Say
2. Look
3. Spell
4. Write
5. Check

1. ride _____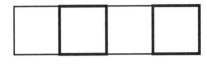

2. nine _____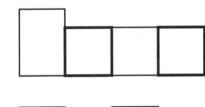

3. five _____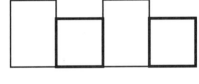

4. hide _____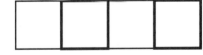

5. mine _____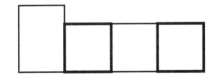

6. time _____

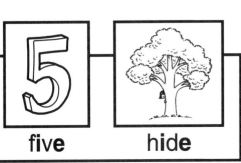

The long **i** sound can be spelled **i__e**.

five   hide

Lesson 25
Core Skills Spelling, Grade 1

Spell and Write

Write the spelling word that completes
each sentence.

ride   hide
nine   mine
five   time

1. Where did the mouse _____?

2. I will share _____ with Mike.

3. What _____ is it?

4. The dog will _____ in the wagon.

5. There are _____ eggs left.

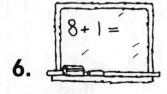

6. Eight and one make _____.

98

Name _____   Date _____

Read and Write

Write the spelling words to complete
the selection.

ride   hide
nine   mine
five   time

A bike contest can test how well you _____.

Don't run and _____. Set up _____

big cones. Ride around them one at a _____.

Ride slowly for four or _____ minutes.

Now you are ready for the contest. You might get to say,

"The prize is _____!"

Practice

Draw lines from the bees to the
hives to make the spelling words.

ride	hide
nine	mine
five	time

ive   ime   ide   ine

Write the words you made.

1. _____   2. _____   3. _____

4. _____   5. _____   6. _____

100

Name _____ Date _____

Lesson 26: More Words with Long i

Say and Write

Study Steps
1. Say
2. Look
3. Spell
4. Write
5. Check

1.  my

2.  by

3.  fly

4.  why

5.  try

6.  cry

The long **i** sound can be spelled **y**.

my   fly

Lesson 26
Core Skills Spelling, Grade 1

Name _____   Date _____

Spell and Write

Write the spelling word that completes
each sentence.

1.   The baby began to _____.

2.   The birds _____ in the sky.

3.   She knows _____ the chair broke.

4.   I put on _____ coat.

5.   He will _____ to skate.

6.   The cat is _____ the door.

Lesson 26
Core Skills Spelling, Grade 1

Name _____ Date _____

Read and Write

Write the spelling words
to complete the story.

my	why
by	try
fly	cry

I made a kite. I made _____ kite from a

bag. I wanted it to _____ up high. People

stood _____ me. They asked _____

I used a bag. I wanted to _____ it. That's

why. The bag did not fly very high, but I did not

_____. I just made another kite.

103

© Houghton Mifflin Harcourt Publishing Company

Lesson 26
Core Skills Spelling, Grade 1

Practice

Add and take away letters.
Write the spelling words.

my	why
by	try
fly	cry

1. [fl] + (y) = _____

2. [w] + [shy] − [s] = _____

3. [m] + (by) − [b] = _____

4. [c] + [dry] − [d] = _____

5. (be) − [e] + [y] = _____

6. [tree] − [ee] + [y] = _____

Name _____ Date _____

Lesson 27: Words with Long o

Study Steps
1. Say
2. Look
3. Spell
4. Write
5. Check

Say and Write

1.  so

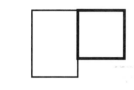

2.  go

3.  old

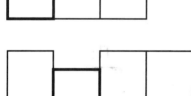

4.  told

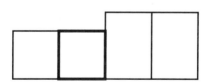

5.  cold

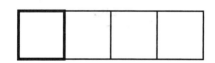

6.  over

The long **o** sound can be spelled **o**.

g**o**

c**o**ld

Lesson 27
Core Skills Spelling, Grade 1

Name _____ Date _____

Spell and Write

Write the spelling word that completes
each sentence.

1. The shop was closed, _____ we left.

2. Jo _____ Bo a joke.

3. The ducks went _____ the water.

4. The ball will _____ far.

5. The man was very _____.

6. The big tree was very _____.

106

Read and Write

Write the spelling words to complete the story.

JoJo wanted to _____ to a special place.

She wanted to go _____ the rainbow. JoJo

packed an _____ bag. She got her coat in

case it was _____. JoJo _____ Gran

about her plan. Gran wanted to go, too, _____

they went together. Good luck, JoJo and Gran!

© Houghton Mifflin Harcourt Publishing Company

Name _____   Date _____

Practice

Write the letter or letters that
complete each spelling word.

1. c ___ l d

2. s ___

3. ___ l d

4. g ___

5. ___ v ___ r

6. t ___ l

Write the words you made.

1. _____   2. _____   3. _____

4. _____   5. _____   6. _____

Name _____ Date _____

Lesson 28: More Words with Long o

Study Steps
1. Say
2. Look
3. Spell
4. Write
5. Check

Say and Write

1. home _____

2. hope _____

3. note _____

4. nose _____

5. road _____

6. coat _____

The long **o** sound can be spelled **o_e** or **oa**.

hom**e**

roa**d**

Spell and Write

Write the spelling word that completes
each sentence.

home	nose
hope	road
note	coat

1. I ride down the _____.

2. We _____ it rains today.

3. My _____ is warm.

4. He has a big _____.

5. Mr. Lo's _____ is on a farm.

6. Joan wrote me a _____.

Name _____ Date _____

Read and Write

Write the spelling words to
complete the story.

home   nose
hope   road
note   coat

One day Mole wanted to take a walk. Dad was not

_____   _____

at _____. Mole wrote Dad a _____.

_____

Then she walked down the _____. She walked

a long way. A cold wind came. Mole's _____

was blue. She wanted her warm _____. "I

_____ I am not lost!" she said. Then Mole saw

her house. She smiled and went inside.

Name _____ Date _____

Practice

Write the letters that spell the long **o** sound.

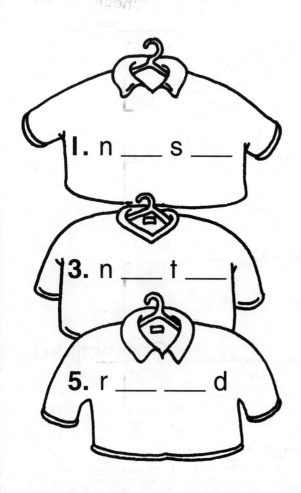

1. n ___ s ___

3. n ___ t ___

5. r ___ ___ d

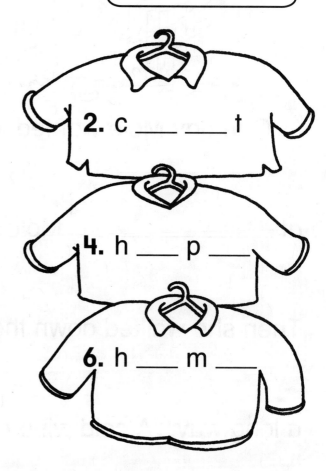

2. c ___ ___ t

4. h ___ p ___

6. h ___ m ___

Write the words you made.

1. _____   **2.** _____   **3.** _____

4. _____   **5.** _____   **6.** _____

112

Name _____ Date _____

Lesson 29: Words with the Vowel Sound in food

Study Steps
1. Say
2. Look
3. Spell
4. Write
5. Check

Say and Write

1. zoo

2. food

3. room

4. moon

5. soon

6. school

The vowel sound in **food** can be spelled **oo**.

zoo

school

113

Spell and Write

Write the spelling word that completes
each sentence.

zoo	moon
food	soon
room	school

1. What jumped over the _____?

2. Where do you go to _____?

3. Molly cleans her _____.

4. It will be dark _____.

5. We had fun at the _____.

6. Jane and Joel shop for _____.

Name _____ Date _____

Read and Write

Write the spelling
words to complete
the story.

Would you like to camp at a _____? At

one zoo, you can sleep in a _____ with beds.

You can sleep under the _____ and stars, too.

You can give _____ to the animals. Your class

from _____ might want to go zoo camping.

Find out about zoo camping _____!

Name _____ Date _____

Practice

Write a spelling word to solve
each riddle.

zoo   moon
food   soon
room   school

 1. I am good for you. What am I?

 2. I am a place where children go. What am I?

 3. I have lots of animals. What am I?

 4. I am a place in your home. What am I?

 5. You can see me at night. What am I?

 6. I mean **before long**. What am I?

1. _____   2. _____   3. _____

4. _____   5. _____   6. _____

116

Name _____ Date _____

Lesson 30: More Words with the Vowel Sound in food

Study Steps
1. Say
2. Look
3. Spell
4. Write
5. Check

Say and Write

1. too _____
2. who _____
3. two _____
4. do _____
5. shoe _____
6. you _____

The vowel sound in **food** can be spelled **oo**, **o**, **oe**, or **ou**.

 tw**o**    t**oo**   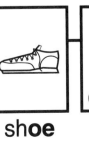 sh**oe**   y**ou**

Lesson 30
Core Skills Spelling, Grade 1

Spell and Write

Write the spelling word that completes
each sentence.

too	do
who	shoe
two	you

1.  It's time to _____ our work.

2.  The hat is _____ big.

3.  Sue, where are _____?

4.  Lou said. "I know _____ you are."

5.  The bike has _____ wheels.

6.  I have gum on my _____.

Name _____ Date _____

Read and Write

Write the spelling words
to complete the selection.

too	do
who	shoe
two	you

Look at your _____ feet. Is there a

_____ on each foot? Shoes keep your feet safe.

Shoes should not be _____ big or too small.

No one knows _____ made the first shoes.

Early people made them from animal skins. Now

_____ can buy shoes in a store. What kind of

shoes _____ you like to wear?

Lesson 30
Core Skills Spelling, Grade 1

Name _____   Date _____

Practice

Write the letter or letters that
complete each spelling word.

too	do
who	shoe
two	you

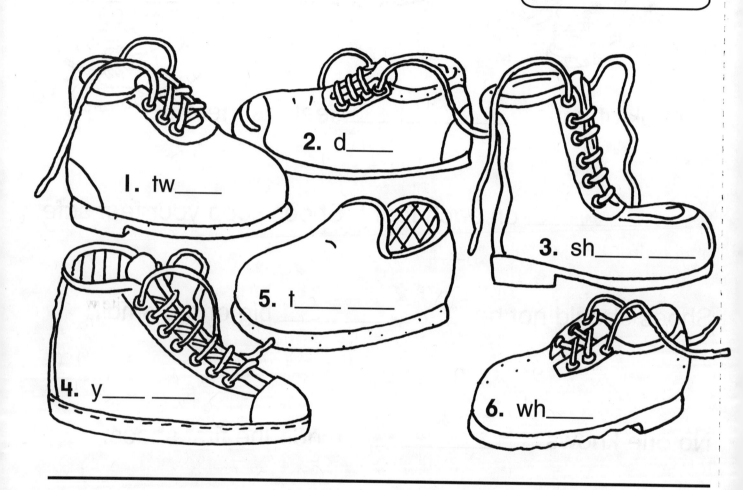

1. tw_____

2. d_____

3. sh_____ _____

4. y_____ _____

5. t_____

6. wh_____

Write the words you made.

1. _____

2. _____

3. _____

4. _____

5. _____

6. _____

Answer Key

Page 1
Children write **m** under these pictures:

1. mat
3. mask
4. mitten
6. moon
7. mouse
8. milk
10. jam
11. drum

Page 2
Children write **d** under these pictures:

1. dad
2. duck
4. doll
5. desk
6. door
7. dig
9. lid
10. sad
12. road

Page 3
Children write **f** under these pictures:

1. feather
2. four
4. fall
5. feet
6. five
7. finger
10. leaf
11. scarf
12. giraffe

Page 4
Children write **g** under these pictures:

1. gas
2. girl
3. game
6. gift
7. goat
8. gate
9. pig
10. dog
12. rug

Page 5
Children write **b** under these pictures:

1. bag
3. bib
4. ball
5. balloon
6. book
8. bed
9. crib
11. globe
12. web

Page 6
Children write **t** under these pictures:

1. tent
2. tub
4. tag
5. top
7. toys
8. tree
9. rat
10. nut
12. bat

Page 7
Children write **s** under these pictures:

1. sock
3. saw
4. soap
5. safe
6. seven
8. soup
10. gas
11. purse
12. glass

Page 8
Children write **w** under these pictures:

1. web
4. well
5. wag
7. wax
10. wet
11. win

Page 9
Children write **k** under these pictures:

1. king
2. kite

121

4. kangaroo

5. kitchen

7. kitten

8. kick

9. hook

10. rake

11. bike

11. rope

12. cap

Page 10
Children write **j**
under these pictures:

1. jar

3. June

6. jug

8. hop

9. jog

11. jet

Page 11
Children write **p**
under these pictures:

1. pen

2. puzzle

4. pillow

5. penny

7. pig

8. pineapple

10. jump

Page 12
Children write **n**
under these pictures:

1. net

2. nap

3. nail

6. note

7. nest

8. nose

9. van

10. pin

11. sun

Page 13
Children write **c**
under these pictures:

1. candle

3. carrots

4. cage

5. cactus

6. corn

8. comb

10. car

11. can

12. coat

Page 14
Children write **h**
under these pictures:

1. ham

2. hen

4. hand

5. hut

7. hop

8. hook

9. hit

10. hill

11. horn

Page 15
Children write **l** under
these pictures:

1. lemon

2. leg

3. lion

5. leaf

6. lid

8. lamb

9. ball

11. doll

12. stool

Page 16
Children write **r**
under these pictures:

1. run

2. rat

4. rock

6. ring

7. rake

8. rose

9. jar

11. star

12. four

Page 17
Children write **v**
under these pictures:

1. vacuum

2. vase

4. vegetables

5. valentine

6. violin

7. vine

10. van

11. volcano

12. vet

122

Page 18
Children write **y**
under these pictures:

1. yell

3. yarn

5. yard

7. yolk

10. yawn

12. yak

Page 19
Children write **z**
under these pictures:

1. zoo

2. zebra

5. zipper

8. zip code

9. zig-zag

11. zero

Page 20
Children write **qu**
under these pictures:

1. queen

3. quart

5. quack

6. quail

Children write **x**
under these pictures:

10. box

11. mix

Page 21
Children write **a**
under these pictures:

1. mask

3. mat

4. bag

5. map

7. hand

8. gas

9. jam

11. man

12. tag

Page 22
Children write **a**
under these pictures
and color them:

1. ham

2. pan

4. map

6. bag

8. hat

9. mat

Page 23
Children circle the
following pictures:

1. can, man

2. wag, tag

3. bat, hat

4. map, clap

5. dad, mad

Page 24

1. fan

2. van

3. pan

4. man

5. can

6. ran

7. bat

8. cat

9. hat

10. mat

11. rat

12. sat

Page 25
Children write **e**
under these pictures:

1. bell

2. dress

4. ten

6. desk

7. pen

8. vest

9. leg

10. nest

11. egg

Page 26
Children write **e**
under these pictures
and color them:

1. vet

2. jet

5. bed

6. net

7. men

9. keg

Page 27
Children circle the
following pictures:

1. sled, shed

2. shell, well

3. peg, keg

4. jet, net

5. men, pen

123

Page 28

1. bell
2. yell
3. tell
4. well
5. fell
6. hen
7. men
8. ten

Page 29

Children write **i** under these pictures:

1. hill
2. six
3. wig
5. lid
7. clip
8. dig
10. fish
11. zip
12. bib

Page 30

Children write **i** under these pictures and color them:

1. pin
3. pig

4. fin
5. dig
8. kit
9. lip

Page 31

Children circle the following pictures:

1. fin, chin
2. sit, hit
3. zip, flip
4. wig, dig
5. mix, six

Page 32

1. hit
2. kit
3. sit
4. dig
5. pig
6. wig
7. big

Page 33

Children write **o** under these pictures:

1. pot
2. mop
3. hop

5. block
6. dot
8. dog
9. lock
11. cot
12. box

Page 34

Children write **o** under these pictures and color them:

1. top
2. fox
5. pop
6. rock
7. log
9. doll

Page 35

Children circle the following pictures:

1. spot, knot
2. ox, box
3. stop, mop
4. lock, block

Page 36

1. hop
2. mop

3. pop
4. cot
5. dot
6. hot
7. pot

Page 37

Children write **u** under these pictures:

1. nut
2. mug
6. bus
7. plug
8. duck
9. up
11. drum
12. truck

Page 38

Children write **u** under these pictures and color them:

1. cup
2. pup
4. sun
6. cub
7. rug
9. nut

Page 39

Children circle the following pictures:

1. cut, nut

2. bun, run

3. scrub, cub

4. plum, drum

5. jug, plug

Page 40

1. mug

2. hug

3. jug

4. bug

5. tug

6. rug

7. cut

8. hut

9. nut

Page 41

Check children's work.

Page 42

1. am

2. can

3. at

4. ran

5. fast

6. last

Page 43

ran, at, fast, last, am, can

Page 44

1. ran

2. last

3. am

4. at

5. can

6. fast

Page 45

Check children's work.

Page 46

1. van

2. that

3. hand

4. sat

5. have

6. has

Page 47

sat, hand, van, has, that, have

Page 48

1. van

2. have

3. hand

4. has

5. sat

6. that

Page 49

Check children's work.

Page 50

1. wet

2. red

3. ten

4. end

5. seven

6. tell

Page 51

red, wet, ten, end, seven, tell

Page 52

1. tell

2. seven

3. ten

4. wet

5. end

6. red

Riddle: letter

Page 53

Check children's work.

Page 54

1. pet

2. when

3. best

4. went

5. get

6. help

Page 55

pet, get, help, when, went, best

Page 56

1. pet

2. when

3. get

4. help

5. went

6. best

125

Page 57

Check children's work.

Page 58

1. sick
2. with
3. is
4. in
5. quit
6. it

Page 59

sick, in, is, it, with, quit

Page 60

1. sick
2. in
3. is
4. quit
5. with
6. it

Page 61

Check children's work.

Page 62

1. six
2. if

3. sit
4. big
5. did
6. this

Page 63

six, big, sit, if, this, did

Page 64

1. big
2. sit
3. six
4. if
5. this
6. did

Page 65

Check children's work.

Page 66

1. hop
2. stop
3. on
4. hot
5. not
6. top

Page 67

hop, on, not, top, stop, hot

Page 68

1. hot
2. on
3. top
4. not
5. stop
6. hop

Page 69

Check children's work.

Page 70

1. sock
2. mop
3. job
4. fox
5. lock
6. box

Page 71

job, mop, fox, box, sock, lock

Page 72

Order of answers may vary.

1. mop

2. sock
3. fox
4. lock
5. job
6. box

Page 73

Check children's work.

Page 74

1. us
2. run
3. jump
4. duck
5. fun
6. much

Page 75

duck, run, fun, jump, much, us

Page 76

1. jump
2. much
3. fun
4. run
5. duck
6. us
7. duck

126

8. much

9. run

10. jump

11. us

12. fun

Page 77
Check children's work.

Page 78
1. bus

2. must

3. cut

4. just

5. but

6. up

Page 79
bus, must, up, but, cut, just

Page 80
1. but

2. just

3. up

4. bus

5. must

6. cut

Page 81
Check children's work.

Page 82
1. make

2. game

3. name

4. same

5. take

6. made

Page 83
name, game, take, same, make, made

Page 84
Order of answers may vary.

1. game

2. same

3. made

4. name

5. take

6. make

Page 85
Check children's work.

Page 86
1. pay

2. day

3. stay

4. may

5. play

6. say

Page 87
day, may, stay, play, say, pay

Page 88
1. play

2. day

3. stay

4. pay

5. say

6. may

Page 89
Check children's work.

Page 90
1. we

2. eat

3. he

4. me

5. be

6. she

Page 91
we, eat, me, she, he, be

Page 92
1. be

2. we

3. he

4. eat

5. me

6. she

Page 93
Check children's work.

Page 94
1. tree

2. street

3. feet

4. see

5. keep

6. three

Page 95
three, street, keep, tree, see, feet

Page 96

1. street
2. tree
3. three
4. see
5. keep
6. feet

Page 97

Check children's work.

Page 98

1. hide
2. mine
3. time
4. ride
5. five
6. nine

Page 99

ride, hide, nine, time, five, mine

Page 100

Order of answers may vary.

1. time
2. five
3. hide

4. ride
5. mine
6. nine

Page 101

Check children's work.

Page 102

1. cry
2. fly
3. why
4. my
5. try
6. by

Page 103

my, fly, by, why, try, cry

Page 104

1. fly
2. why
3. my
4. cry
5. by
6. try

Page 105

Check children's work.

Page 106

1. so
2. told
3. over
4. go
5. cold
6. old

Page 107

go, over, old, cold, told, so

Page 108

1. cold
2. so
3. old
4. go
5. over
6. told

Page 109

Check children's work.

Page 110

1. road
2. hope
3. coat
4. nose
5. home
6. note

Page 111

home, note, road, nose, coat, hope

Page 112

1. nose
2. coat
3. note
4. hope
5. road
6. home

Page 113

Check children's work.

Page 114

1. moon
2. school
3. room
4. soon

5. zoo

6. food

Page 115

zoo, room, moon,
food, school, soon

Page 116

1. food

2. school

3. zoo

4. room

5. moon

6. soon

Page 117

Check children's
work

Page 118

1. do

2. too

3. you

4. who

5. two

6. shoe

Page 119

two, shoe, too, who,
you, do

Page 120

1. two

2. do

3. shoe

4. you

5. too

6. who

© Houghton Mifflin Harcourt Publishing Company

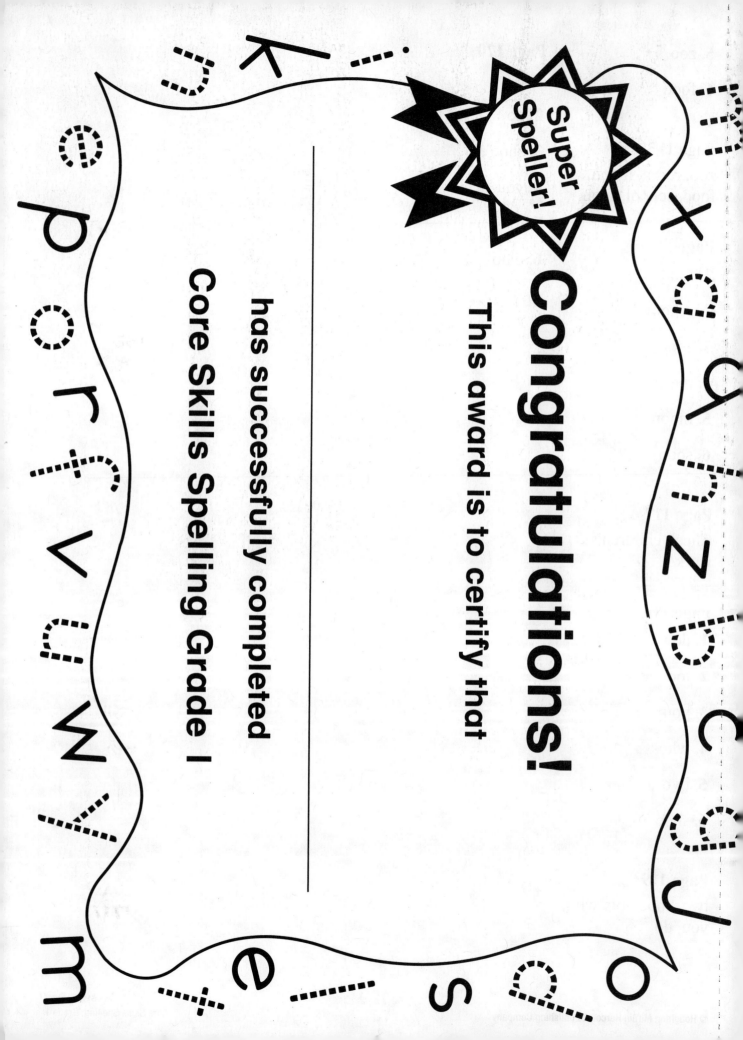

Super Speller!

Congratulations!

This award is to certify that

_____

has successfully completed

Core Skills Spelling Grade 1